MOTHER TERESA

Published by Creative Education
123 South Broad Street
Mankato, Minnesota 56001
Creative Education is an imprint of The Creative Company.

DESIGN AND PRODUCTION **EVANSDAY DESIGN**

PHOTOGRAPHS BY Corbis (BALDEV/CORBIS SYGMA, Bettmann, CORBIS SYGMA,
Owen Franken, Michael Freeman, Jeremy Horner, Hulton-Deutsch Collec-
tion, JP Laffont/Sygma, ROUGEMONT MAURICE/CORBIS SYGMA, Reuters, Brad-
ley Smith, Peter Turnley), Getty Images (Sal Dimarco Jr., Francois Lochon)

Excerpted from *No Greater Love* by Mother Teresa, ISBN 1-57731-006-3, ©
2002. Reprinted with permission of New World Library.
www.newworldlibrary.com

LIBRARY OF CONGRESS CATALOGING-IN-PUBLICATION DATA
Fitzpatrick, Anne.
Mother Teresa / by Anne Fitzpatrick.
p. cm. — (Genius)
Summary: An account of the life of Mother Teresa, the Serbian nun who
founded a religious order, the Sisters of Charity, to serve the sick and needy
of Calcutta, India, and of the work that earned her a Nobel Peace Prize.
ISBN 1-58341-330-8
1. Teresa, Mother, 1910-—Juvenile literature. 2. Missionaries of charity—Biography—Juvenile literature. 3. Nuns—India—Calcutta—Biography—Juvenile
literature. [1. Teresa, Mother, 1910- 2. Missionaries of Charity. 3. Missionaries. 4. Nuns. 5. Nobel Prizes—Biography. 6. Women—Biography.] I. Title. II.
Genius (Mankato, Minn.)

BX4406.5.Z8F58 2004
271'.97—dc22   2003065228

First edition

9 8 7 6 5 4 3 2 1

[M O T H E R   T E R E S A]

GENiUS

Anne Fitzpatrick

MOTHER TERESA, A WOMAN WHO RARELY SLEPT

MORE THAN FOUR HOURS A NIGHT, WHOSE LUMINOUS SMILE COULD

SWAY PEOPLE TO HER WILL OR FILL THEM WITH THE AWARENESS

OF GOD'S LOVE, AND WHO BY HER UNSHAKEABLE FAITH WORKED

UNCOUNTED MIRACLES, WAS MYSTIFIED BY THE CURIOSITY SO MANY

PEOPLE HAD ABOUT HER PERSONAL JOURNEY. WITH BREATHTAKING

HUMILITY, SHE SAW THE AWE WITH WHICH THE WORLD VIEWED HER AS

NOTEWORTHY ONLY IN THAT IT MIGHT BRING PEOPLE CLOSER TO GOD.

"No one thinks of the pen while reading a letter;
they only want to know the mind of the person who
wrote the letter. That's exactly what I am in God's
hand—a little pencil. God is writing his love letter
to the world in this way, through works of love."

MOTHER TERESA

GENiUS

1 THE CALL TO GOD

MOTHER TERESA WAS BORN AGNES GONXHA BOJAXHIU ON AUGUST 26, 1910, IN SKOPJE, ALBANIA. HER FATHER, NIKOLA BOJAXHIU, WAS A WELL-TO-DO MERCHANT AND A LEADING MEMBER OF THE COMMUNITY. HER MOTHER, DRANAFILE BOJAXHIU, WAS A TRADITIONAL WIFE AND MOTHER WHO ALWAYS SET ASIDE HER WORK AND PUT ON A CLEAN DRESS TO GREET HER HUSBAND WHEN HE CAME HOME.

A group of Albanian refugees in 1912

The three Bojaxhiu children—daughter Aga, son Lazar, and the youngest, Agnes—were raised with firm but loving discipline, guided by a strong Catholic faith.

Although Nikola was a stern father with high expectations for his children, his return from frequent travels was always eagerly anticipated, both for the gifts he would bring and the wonderful stories he could tell. But in 1919, when Agnes was eight years old, he returned from a trip suddenly and gravely ill. He died shortly thereafter. This was a time of intense fighting in Albania between Serbia, Greece, Austria, and other surrounding countries, and Albania was struggling to maintain its independence. Nikola was very involved in Albanian nationalism, and many people suspected that his death was caused by poisoning.

Nikola's business partner seized the assets of their construction supply store, leaving Drana and her children with very little. Drana began sewing, embroidering, and selling cloth to support

MOTHER TERESA IS BORN AGNES GONXHA BOJAXHIU IN SKOPJE, ALBANIA (NOW IN PRESENT-DAY MACEDONIA), ON AUGUST 26. *Timeline* **1910**

7

her family. But despite their new poverty, the family's commitment to charity did not falter. The poor had always been welcome at their table. Drana never sent anyone away empty-handed. When Lazar asked her who the people eating with them were, she replied, "Some of them are your relations, but all of them are our people."

"Sometimes my mother and sisters gave the impression that they lived inside the church, going to the principal religious events and the missionary talks that so interested Gonxha [Mother Teresa] above all."

LAZAR BOJAXHIU

Drana was an extremely devout woman. The family prayed together every evening and attended church regularly. Drana took Agnes and the others with her when she visited the elderly and sick to wash and feed them. She told her children, "When you do good, do it quietly, as if you were throwing a stone into the sea."

Albania was primarily a Muslim country; the Bojaxhiu family was among the approximately 10 percent of the population who were Catholic. They attended church at the Sacred Heart, where Agnes and Aga were known as "the two nightingales" for their beautiful singing in the church choir. Agnes was very active in the church. The small, dark-haired girl had large, deep-set eyes and often wore a serious expression. She was described as a popular, fun-loving child who had many friends, but she was shy with boys and at times seemed withdrawn and introverted.

"I wasn't more than 12 years old when, in the bosom of my family, I felt a strong desire to belong to God," Mother Teresa later recalled. Yet Agnes sometimes dreamed of being a writer or musician. She did well in school, even tutoring her classmates. She published two articles in the local paper. She also loved to read and write poetry. When Agnes was 15 or 16, she asked one of the priests at Sacred Heart how she

Timeline **1919** NIKOLA BOJAXHIU, AGNES'S FATHER, DIES SUDDENLY.

This 1915 photograph shows Albanian soldiers drilling for war; Mother Teresa's father, Nikola Bojaxhiu, was very devoted to the Albanian cause.

Timeline **1928**   AGNES LEAVES HOME TO BECOME A NUN IN THE LORETO ORDER OF IRELAND.

could know whether God was truly calling her. He told her that if something fills you with joy, then it is from God.

At Sacred Heart, Agnes had access to many magazines about missionary work, such as *Catholic Mission*. As a child, she had wanted to help the poor of Africa, but now she became particularly interested in a group of Albanian priests on a mission to India. She followed news about them and other missionaries in India eagerly. When the priests wrote about the work being done by the Loreto sisters, an Irish order (community) of nuns, Agnes's mind was made up.

Seventeen-year-old Agnes told her mother that she wanted to join the Loreto sisters and work with the poor in India. At first Drana refused to allow it. She later said that she wanted to test the strength of her daughter's commitment to the religious life. Agnes held her ground, and Drana gave Agnes her blessing, with one condition: Agnes must be "only, all for God and Jesus." In later years, Mother Teresa said, "If I had not been true to my vocation she would have judged me as God would judge me. One day she will ask me, 'Have you lived only, all for God?'"

AGNES ARRIVES IN INDIA AND BECOMES A LORETO NOVICE. *Timeline* **1929**

Calcutta, India, has long been host to thousands of homeless people; in this photograph taken in 1950, homeless Calcuttans sleep out on the street.

2

ONLY, ALL FOR GOD

A sacred cow drinking from a street fountain

Once Betika arrived, Agnes took leave of her mother and sister and made the first of many journeys into the unknown with only her faith to guide her.

Agnes and Betika stayed at Loreto Abbey in Dublin, Ireland, for six weeks, spending most of their time learning English. They were forbidden to speak to each other in their native language so that they might learn English more quickly. After this introduction to the Loreto order, the two young women boarded a ship for India.

The voyage took more than a month. Agnes wrote in *Catholic Mission* that the journey became much easier once a priest joined them in Columbo, Sri Lanka: "So now we had mass daily, and life on board no longer seemed so desolate to us." Their first landfall in India was in Madras. Agnes was shocked at the poverty she saw there. She wrote home, "If our people could only see all this, they would stop grumbling about their own misfortunes and offer thanks to God for blessing them with such abundance."

SISTER TERESA TAKES VOWS OF POVERTY, CHASTITY, AND OBEDIENCE FOR LIFE, BECOMING MOTHER TERESA.   *Timeline* **1937**

Agnes became a novice on May 23, 1929, donning the black habit, or dress, and veil of a Loreto sister. Along with the veil, the 18-year-old took the name Sister Mary Teresa of the Child Jesus, after St. Therese of Lisieux, who wrote of "doing the least of actions for love." Agnes's novitiate was spent in Darjeeling, a small town in the foothills of the Himalayas. After this period of training was completed, she went to the Loreto convent in Calcutta.

The Loreto order was primarily dedicated to teaching, and Sister Teresa loved her work. She taught geography and history in the high school attached to the convent. The convent was next to the slums of Motijhil, where Teresa would one day work among the poorest of the poor, but it was surrounded by high walls. Nonetheless, Teresa visited the slums every Sunday, taking whatever gifts of food or clothing she could find.

In 1937, 27-year-old Sister Teresa became Mother Teresa, according to Loreto custom, when she took her final vows of poverty, chastity, and obedience for life. She was very happy in her new life, and she was doing much good. Yet the awareness that her path lay beyond Loreto may already have begun to surface. In 1943, in response to a letter in which Teresa had spoken of her love for teaching, her mother wrote: "Dear child, do not forget that you went to India for the sake of the poor."

The call to leave Loreto and dedicate herself to the poorest of the poor came on September 10, 1946. Mother Teresa was on a train on her way to an annual retreat in

"Something of God's universal love has rubbed off on Mother Teresa, giving her homely features a noticeable luminosity; a shining quality. She has lived so closely with her Lord that the same enchantment clings about her that sent the crowds chasing after him in Jerusalem and Galilee; and made his mere presence seem a harbinger of healing."

MALCOLM MUGGERIDGE
BRITISH JOURNALIST

Timeline **1946**   MOTHER TERESA RECEIVES HER "CALL WITHIN A CALL" TO LEAVE THE CONVENT AND SERVE THE POOR.

Located at the base of the Himalayan Mountains, Darjeeling, India, was the place where Mother Teresa trained for 17 years to become a nun.

Timeline **1948**   MOTHER TERESA IS GRANTED PERMISSION TO LEAVE THE LORETO ORDER TO WORK AMONG CALCUTTA'S POOR.

Darjeeling. The message was clear: "I was to leave the convent and help the poor while living among them. It was an order. To fail it would have been to break the faith." Once again, Mother Teresa heard God calling her to leave everything she knew and trust to faith alone.

As when her mother at first refused to allow her to join the Loreto sisters, Mother Teresa had to demonstrate the strength of her commitment and faith in this second call. "I knew that it was His will," she said, "and that I had to follow Him. There was no doubt that it was going to be His work. But I waited for the decision of the Church."

It would be two years before Mother Teresa was given permission to leave the convent for a trial period of one year. She would continue to be a nun, bound by her vows and subject to the guidance of the Archbishop of Calcutta, but she was released from the cloistered life of the Loreto order to work among the poorest of the poor. "To leave Loreto was my greatest sacrifice," she later said, "the most difficult thing I have ever done. It was much more difficult than to leave my family and my country to enter religious life. Loreto, my spiritual training, my work there, meant everything to me."

MOTHER TERESA OPENS A SCHOOL IN A DIRT YARD IN MOTIJHIL, A SLUM DISTRICT OF CALCUTTA.   *Timeline* **1948**

After periods of deep reflection and prayer, Mother Teresa felt called to rededicate her life to helping the poor, which meant leaving her beloved Loreto.

YOU DID IT TO ME

ON AUGUST 16, 1948, 37-YEAR-OLD MOTHER TERESA LEFT HER LIFE AT LORETO BEHIND. SHE EXCHANGED HER BLACK HABIT FOR A SIMPLE WHITE AND BLUE SARI, A TRADITIONAL INDIAN DRESS, CHOSEN FOR ITS CHEAPNESS. CLUTCHING A TRAIN TICKET AND FIVE RUPEES (ABOUT 55 U.S. CENTS), SHE SET OUT ON HER JOURNEY OF FAITH.

Outside Mother Teresa's home for the dying

After a few weeks of basic medical training in Para, India, Mother Teresa returned to Calcutta and moved into a small room in a home for the elderly run by the Little Sisters of the Poor. Early one morning, she caught a bus to Motijhil, the neighborhood outside her old convent of Loreto. The overwhelming poverty of the slums must have filled the young woman, alone and inexperienced, with fear and doubt. The children were half-naked and starving, and the streets were filled with raw sewage, insects, and disease. But she set to work in the way she knew best. Gathering five children in a small yard, she began to teach them the alphabet, scratching the letters in the dirt with a stick. The very next day, she had twice as many children to teach. In addition to the alphabet, she taught them hygiene and needlework, and took them with her to visit the sick.

Several of Mother Teresa's former students and fellow teachers from Loreto came to help her teach in the slums. Some of them were inspired by her passion to join her in a life of poverty. In April

1950, Mother Teresa submitted the rules she had written for this new community of women to Church officials in Rome as the Constitutions of the Missionary Sisters of Charity.

According to the Constitutions, the sisters were to devote themselves body and soul to serving the poorest of the poor, and to do so with joy and love—with the awareness that Christ was in each person. Mother Teresa quoted one of her favorite lines of scripture to explain the philosophy of her order: "We believe what Jesus has said: 'I was hungry, I was naked, I was homeless; I was unwanted, unloved, uncared-for—and you did it to me.'" The Constitutions were approved, and the first group of novices, including Mother Teresa, made their vows in April 1953.

One day in 1952, Mother Teresa came upon a woman lying on the street, half eaten by rats and ants. It was not an uncommon sight in the crowded streets of Calcutta's slums. Mother Teresa carried her to a hospital, but it refused to take the woman because it could do nothing for her. She went to the local authorities and asked for a place where she could take in people who were dying in such poverty and loneliness that they had nowhere to go. They gave her two unused rooms in a temple dedicated to Kali, the Hindu goddess of death and fertility. There Mother Teresa founded Nirmal Hriday. Although some of its residents are nursed back to health, that is not its primary purpose: "We want them [the dying] to know that there are people who really love

"No priest was ever going to tell her how to do things differently; she absolutely knew herself and she brooked no opposition or interference, and if she wanted something done she would carry on, telephoning or seeing people until it was done, and that was really the secret of her success."

ANNE SEBBA
BIOGRAPHER

Timeline **1950**   THE MISSIONARIES OF CHARITY ORDER IS FOUNDED.

This Indian boy was in danger of starvation as he begged for food on the streets of Calcutta in 1943; to this day, thousands of people die of starvation in India.

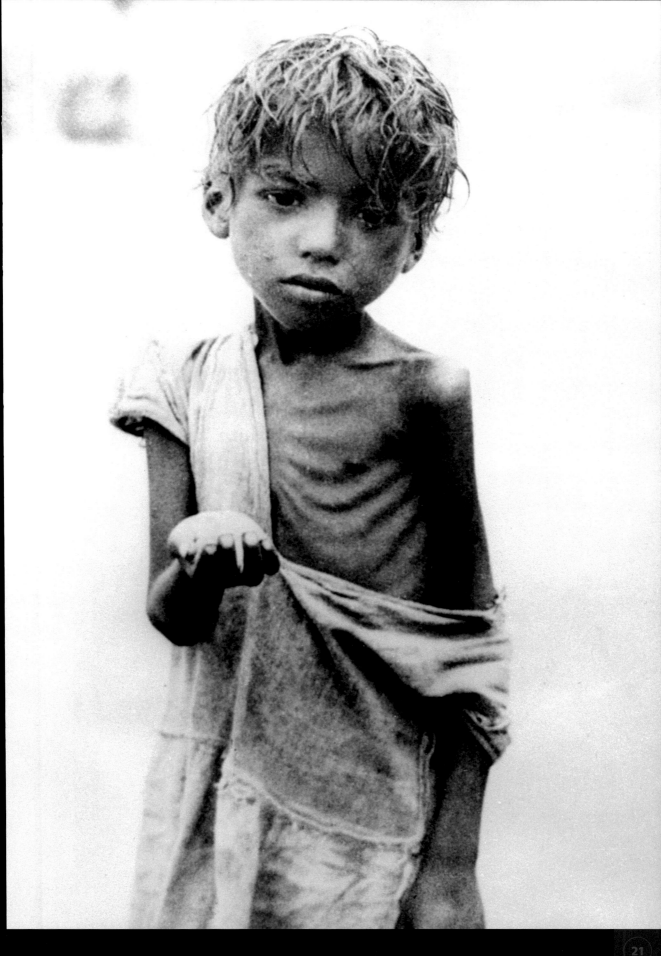

them, who really want them, at least for the few hours they have to live, to know human and divine love," Mother Teresa explained.

By this time, Mother Teresa was renting the top floor of a house for a convent. It was quickly becoming too small, and in 1953, the sisters moved into the building that remains their mother house, or headquarters, today. It is a large house, likely the former home of a wealthy family, surrounding a stone courtyard. The chapel on the second floor is a long, bare room with windows on one side. The noise of the street fills the house at all hours, even during prayers. Each morning, after waking at 4:30 A.M. for prayer and meditation, mass, washing, chores, and breakfast, the Missionaries of Charity go their separate ways. Some go to Nirmal Hriday, to wash and feed the dying, or to Shishu Bavan, founded in 1955, where abandoned children are given the chance to feel loved; others go to Shanti Nagar, a community of lepers founded in 1964, where they dispense medicine and train the lepers to support themselves. Wherever they go, the sisters serve with joy and love, following the example set by Mother Teresa.

THE FIRST MISSIONARY SISTERS OF CHARITY, INCLUDING MOTHER TERESA, TAKE THEIR VOWS. | *Timeline* **1953**

Mother Teresa created a new order—the Missionary Sisters of Charity—that would help the sick, poor, and abandoned "with the awareness that Christ was in each person."

4 A QUIET STORM

THE CALL THAT MOTHER TERESA HEARD ON THE TRAIN IN DARJEELING WAS ANSWERED BY MANY MORE YOUNG WOMEN. BY 1960, THE MISSIONARIES OF CHARITY HAD OPENED 25 HOUSES IN INDIA. IN 1965, CHURCH AUTHORITIES GRANTED THEM PERMISSION TO EXPAND INTERNATIONALLY. THE FIRST MISSIONARIES OF CHARITY HOME OUTSIDE OF INDIA WAS OPENED IN COCOROTE, VENEZUELA, THAT SAME YEAR.

Mother Teresa with Calcuttan children

Within 10 years, 24 more houses were opened in 14 countries, including the United States, Italy, Ethiopia, and Britain. "As long as God gives me vocations," Mother Teresa said, "it's a sign that God wants the work to spread, and wherever there are poor, we shall go and serve them."

But young women with a desire to serve the poor were not the only people to heed Mother Teresa's call. Thanks in part to a television interview by a well-known British journalist, she was quickly achieving a level of fame not normally associated with a nun. In 1979, she received the ultimate recognition: it was announced that Mother Teresa, from whom "the most wretched have received compassion without condescension," would be awarded the Nobel Peace Prize.

When she arrived in Oslo, Norway, to receive the prize, a journalist asked her why she had come in person, despite her dislike of being the center of attention. She replied, "I am myself unworthy

THE FIRST MISSIONARIES OF CHARITY CHILDREN'S HOME, SHISHU BAVAN, IS OPENED. *Timeline* **1955** of the prize. I do not want it personally. But by this award the Norwegian people have recognized the existence of the poor. It is on their behalf that I have come."

Mother Teresa accepted the prize on December 10, 1979, at the age of 69. Standing in the Great Hall of the University of Oslo, before hundreds of people, as well as television cameras and journalists, she spoke without notes or preparation, as was her custom. The tiny woman bore the rapt attention of the crowd with a straightforward calmness. She began with a sign of the cross and asked her audience to join her in saying the prayer of St. Francis: "Lord, make me an instrument of thy peace...."

A threadbare coat was buttoned over her white and blue sari, and she wore wool socks, borrowed at the insistence of a Norwegian nun, on her sandaled feet. Her only decorations in that bejeweled assembly were the crucifix that pinned her sari at the shoulder, the rosary she clasped in her hands, and the joyous smile that transformed her sun-darkened, wrinkled face into a vision of beauty.

She spoke as if each person in the room was alone with her, conversing intimately. "And so here I am talking with you," she said. "I want you to find the poor here, right in your own home first. And begin love there. Be that good news to your own people. And find out about your next-door neighbor. Do you know who they are?"

"What stunned everyone was her energy. She saw the problem, fell to her knees, prayed for a few seconds, and then she was rattling off a list of supplies she needed.... We didn't expect a saint to be so efficient. She was a cross between a military commander and St. Francis."

RED CROSS OFFICIAL IN BEIRUT

"She is tiny to look at, but there is nothing small about her. To meet her is to feel utterly humble, to sense the power of tenderness and the strength of love."

INDIRA GANDHI
FORMER PRIME MINISTER OF INDIA

Timeline **1965** THE FIRST MISSIONARIES OF CHARITY HOUSE OUTSIDE OF INDIA IS OPENED IN COCOROTE, VENEZUELA.

Mother Teresa received the 1979 Nobel Peace Prize in Oslo, Norway, and then moved the crowd with a heartfelt acceptance speech against abortion.

Unabashed by the power represented in the people assem-
bled before her, unbowed by the greatness of the gift she had
been given, Mother Teresa spoke simply and sincerely of what
was nearest her heart. Even on such a day, she was not afraid
to broach a controversial subject: "I feel the greatest destroyer
of the peace today is abortion, because it is a direct war, a direct killing, direct murder by the mother herself.... Because if a
mother can kill her own child, what is left but for me to kill you
and you to kill me?" Even this passionate speech about one of
the most violently controversial issues in the world today was
accepted without objection because it was given sincerely, by one who lived the
words she spoke.

At Mother Teresa's request, the prize banquet was canceled, and the money that
would have been spent on it was added to her prize money. According to Mother
Teresa, she could feed 400 people for a year on the cost of the banquet alone. She
planned to use the prize money to build housing for the homeless and lepers.

The next day, a Norwegian journalist wrote, "How good it is to experience the
world press for once spellbound by a real star, with a real glitter, a star without a
wig, without a painted face, without false eyelashes, without a mink and without
diamonds, without theatrical gestures and airs. Her only thought is how to use the
Nobel Prize in the best possible way for the world's poorest of the poor."

MOTHER TERESA ACCEPTS THE NOBEL PEACE PRIZE "IN THE NAME OF THE POOR, THE HUNGRY, THE SICK, AND THE LONELY." Timeline 1979

In this 1979 photo, Mother Teresa cradles a baby that has been named for her;
the Nobel Prize brought Mother Teresa's noble deeds to the fore of the world's consciousness.

5 SOMETHING BEAUTIFUL FOR GOD

MOTHER TERESA ONCE SAID THAT SHE HAD MADE A BARGAIN WITH GOD, THAT A SOUL WOULD BE RELEASED FROM PURGATORY FOR EVERY PHOTOGRAPH THAT WAS TAKEN OF HER. SHE WAS VERY UNCOMFORTABLE WITH THE ATTENTION THAT BECAME MORE AND MORE INTENSE THROUGHOUT HER LATER YEARS. NONETHELESS, SHE RECOGNIZED THAT THROUGH HER, THE POOR WERE GAINING RECOGNITION, AND PEOPLE ALL OVER THE WORLD WERE HEARING ABOUT GOD.

Guerrillas fighting in Beirut, Lebanon

Fame brought her increasing opportunities to do God's work. In 1982, Pope John Paul II sent her to Beirut, Lebanon, to express support for victims of the war being fought there by the Israeli army and Palestinian guerrilla fighters. Once there, she heard of a group of mentally handicapped children trapped in the war zone. The bombing and shelling were at their worst, and there were snipers everywhere. After a prolonged argument with local officials, representatives from the Red Cross, the clergymen who had accompanied her, and every other voice of reason, Mother Teresa announced that she would pray for a cease-fire. At 4:00 P.M. she began to pray; by 5:00 P.M. the city was suddenly quiet. Under Mother Teresa's supervision, 38 terrified children were evacuated from the war zone, and arrangements were made for their care.

MOTHER TERESA VISITS BEIRUT, LEBANON, DURING FIGHTING BETWEEN ISRAELI SOLDIERS AND PALESTINIAN GUERRILLAS. *Timeline* **1982**

But her fame could not open every door. Mother Teresa was not able to return to her homeland until 1991, when Albania's communist regime had finally begun to collapse. Her repeated attempts to arrange exit visas for her mother and sister, trapped inside, had failed. She was told that while she could enter the country to see them, there was no guarantee that she would be allowed to leave. In order to see her mother, she would have had to give up the work she was doing for the poor. Drana and Aga died in 1972 and 1973, respectively. Visiting their graves was one of the few occasions on which Mother Teresa was seen to weep.

She could seem superhuman while she worked tirelessly for her beloved poor, but as Mother Teresa grew older, her fragile humanity began to show more and more. She was hospitalized several times, and in 1989, she was fitted with a pacemaker for her overworked heart. The constant travel required to visit more than 500 communities of the Missionaries of Charity in more than 100 countries was an increasing burden. In 1990, Mother Teresa requested and received permission from the pope to step down as Superior General of the order, prompting much speculation about who could fill her shoes. But the Missionaries of Charity General Council chose instead to reelect Mother Teresa, who had just turned 80 years old. "I had expected to be free, but God has His own plans," she

"Today the opportunity offers itself to us of welcoming the presence of truly the most powerful woman on earth.... she is much more important than I am or than all of us are. She is the United Nations! She is the peace of the world!"

JAVIER PEREZ DE CUELLAR
FORMER SECRETARY GENERAL
OF THE UNITED NATIONS

"What wonderful work this little woman knew how to do with the strength of faith in God and love for her neighbor! Mother Teresa was God's gift to the poorest of the poor and at the same time ...she was and remains a remarkable gift for the Church and for the world."

POPE JOHN PAUL II

Throughout history, children have been forced into fighting; Mother Teresa's visit to Beirut, Lebanon, brought about the evacuation of 38 children from a war zone.

> *"I suppose the simplest explanation for the great popularity of Mother Teresa is that, in a world of structures and technology in which no person seems to matter very much, she has affirmed the preciousness of human life."*
>
> ABIGAIL McCARTHY
> AMERICAN COLUMNIST

said. "It is God's will and we have to do what He wants from us. God's work will continue with great love."

Mother Teresa continued to carry out God's work until she finally "went home to God" on September 5, 1997. A Missionaries of Charity ambulance with "Mother" written across the windshield carried her body to a church where crowds of people eager to say good-bye could see her. Her funeral was carried out with all of the grandeur of one of India's most celebrated citizens. The same carriage that had carried the body of Mahatma Gandhi carried Mother Teresa through the streets of Calcutta. The ceremony was held in a stadium and attended by some of the world's most powerful leaders. She was buried under a simple stone slab near the Missionaries of Charity mother house, in the neighborhood in which she had worked for so long and with so much success to create "something beautiful for God."

Since Mother Teresa's burial in the Mother House of the Missionaries of Charity, her grave has become a place of pilgrimage for people of all faiths.

IN HER

WORDS

IN THE FOLLOWING ESSAYS, MOTHER TERESA USES PERSONAL STORIES AND BIBLICAL REFERENCES TO EXPLAIN THE GREAT IMPORTANCE OF LOVING ONE ANOTHER, HAVING COMPASSION FOR THE POOR AND DYING, AND GIVING OF ONESELF TO THOSE IN NEED. IN HER OWN WORDS, MOTHER TERESA'S DEEP COMMITMENT TO SPREADING GOD'S MESSAGE OF LOVE AND FORGIVENESS THROUGH EVERY WORD AND ACTION SHINES THOUGH WITH HUMILITY, HONESTY, AND—MOST OF ALL—LOVE.

ON LOVE *Jesus came into this world for one purpose. He came to give us the good news that God loves us, that God is love, that He loves you, and He loves me. How did Jesus love you and me? By giving His life.*

God loves us with a tender love. That is all that Jesus came to teach us: the tender love of God. "I have called you by your name, you are mine" (Isaiah 43:1 NAB).

The whole gospel is very, very simple. Do you love me? Obey my commandments. He's turning and twisting just to get around to one thing: love one another.

"Thou shalt love the Lord thy God with thy whole heart, with thy whole soul, and with all thy mind" (Deuteronomy 6:5 KJV). This is the command of our great God, and He cannot command the impossible. Love is a fruit, in season at all times and within the reach of every hand. Anyone may gather it and no limit is set.

Everyone can reach this love through meditation, the spirit of prayer, and sacrifice, by an intense interior life. Do not think that love, in order to be genuine, has to be extraordinary.

I have experienced many human weaknesses, many human frailties, and I still experience them. But we need to use them. We need to work for Christ with a humble heart, with the humility of Christ. He comes and uses us to be His love and compassion in the world in spite of our weaknesses and frailties.

One day I picked up a man from the gutter. His body was covered with worms. I brought him to our house, and what did this man say? He did not curse. He did not blame anyone. He just said, "I've lived like an animal in the street, but I'm going to die like an angel, loved and cared for!" It took us three hours to clean him. Finally, the man looked up at the sister and said, "Sister, I'm going home to God." And then he died. I've never seen such a radiant smile on a human face as the one I saw on that man's face. He went home to God. See what love can do! It is possible that young sister did not think about it at the moment, but she was touching the body of Christ. Jesus said so when He said, "As often as you did it for one of my least brothers, you did it for me" (Matthew 25:40 RSV). And this is where you and I fit into God's plan.

I feel that we too often focus only on the negative aspect of life—on what is bad. If we were more willing to see the good and the beautiful things that surround us, we would be able to transform our families. From there, we would change our next-door neighbors and then others who live in our neighborhood or city. We would be able to bring peace and love to our world, which hungers so much for these things.

If we really want to conquer the world, we will not be able to do it with bombs or with other weapons of destruction. Let us conquer the world with our love. Let us interweave our lives with bonds of sacrifice and love, and it will be possible for us to conquer the world.

We do not need to carry out grand things in order to show a great love for God and for our neighbor. It is the intensity of love we put into our gestures that makes them into something beautiful for God.

Peace and war start within one's own home. If we really want peace for the world, let us start by loving one another within our families. Sometimes it is hard for us to smile at one another. It is often difficult for the husband to smile at his wife or for the wife to smile at her husband.

In order for love to be genuine, it has to be above all a love for our neighbor. We must love those who are nearest to us, in our own family. From there, love spreads toward whoever may need us.

It is easy to love those who live far away. It is not always easy to love those who live right next to us. It is easier to offer a dish of rice to meet the hunger of a needy person than to comfort the loneliness and the anguish of someone in our own home who does not feel loved.

I want you to go and find the poor in your homes. Above all, your love has to start there. I want you to be the good news to those around you. I want you to be concerned about your next-door neighbor. Do you know who your neighbor is?

True love is love that causes us pain, that hurts; and yet brings us joy. That is why we must pray to God and ask Him to give us the courage to love.

—————————

ON GIVING   I will tell you a story. One night a man came to our house and told me, "There is a family with eight children. They have not eaten for days."

I took some food with me and went. When I came to that family, I saw the faces of those little children disfigured by hunger. There was no sorrow or sadness in their faces, just the deep pain of hunger. I gave the rice to the mother. She divided the rice in two, and went out, carrying half the rice. When she came back, I asked her, "Where did you go?" She gave me this simple answer, "To my neighbors; they are hungry also!" I was not surprised that she gave—poor people are really very generous. I was surprised that she knew they were hungry. As a rule, when we are suffering, we are so focused on ourselves, we have no time for others.

━━━━━━━━━━━━━━━━

Here in Calcutta we have a number of non-Christians and Christians who work together in the house of the dying and other places. There are also some who offer their care to the lepers. One day an Australian man came and made a substantial donation. But as he did this he said, "This is something external. Now I want to give something of myself." He now comes regularly to the house of the dying to shave the sick men and to converse with them. This man gives not only his money but also his time. He could have spent it on himself, but what he wants is to give himself.

I often ask for gifts that have nothing to do with money. There are always things one can get. What I desire is the presence of the donor, for him to touch those to whom he gives, for him to smile at them, to pay attention to them.

If our poor die of hunger, it is not because God does not care for them. Rather, it is because neither you nor I are generous enough. It is because we are not instruments of love in the hands of God. We do not recognize Christ when once again He appears to us in the hungry man, in the lonely woman, in the child who is looking for a place to get warm.

━━━━━━━━━━━━━━━━

Have you ever experienced the joy of giving? I do not want you to give to me from your abundance. I never allow people to have fund-raisers for me. I don't want that. I want you to give of yourself. The love you put into the giving is the most important thing.

I don't want people donating just to get rid of something. There are people in Calcutta who have so much money that they want to get rid of it. They sometimes have money to spare, money that they try to hide.

A few days ago I received a package wrapped in plain paper. I thought that it might contain stamps, cards, or something like that, so I put it aside. I planned to open it later when I had the time. A few hours later I opened it without even suspecting its contents. It was hard for me to believe my eyes. That package contained twenty thousand rupees. It didn't have a return address or any note, which made me think that it might be money owed to the government.

I don't like people to send me something because they want to get rid of it. Giving is something different. It is sharing.

I also don't want you to give me what you have left over. I want you to give from your want until you really feel it!

The other day I received fifteen dollars from a man who has been paralyzed for twenty years. The paralysis only allows him the use of his right hand. The only company he tolerates is tobacco. He told me, "I have stopped smoking for a week. I'm sending you the money I've saved from not buying cigarettes." It must have been a horrible sacrifice for him. I bought bread with his money, and I gave it to those who were hungry. So both the giver and those who received experienced joy.

This is something all of us need to learn. The chance to share our love with others is a gift from God. May it be for us just as it was for Jesus. Let's love one another as He has loved us. Let's love one another with undivided love. Let's experience the joy of loving God and loving one another.

One thing will always secure heaven for us: the acts of charity and kindness with which we have filled our lives. We will never know how much good just a simple smile can do. We tell people how kind, forgiving, and understanding God is, but are we the living proof? Can they really see this kindness, this forgiveness, this understanding alive in us?

Let us be very sincere in our dealings with each other and have the courage to accept each other as we are. Do not be surprised or become preoccupied at each other's failure; rather see and find the good in each other, for each one of us is created in the image of God. Keep in mind that our community is not composed of those who are already saints, but of those who are trying to become saints. Therefore, let us be extremely patient with each other's faults and failures.

Use your tongue for the good of others, for out of the abundance of the heart the mouth speaks. We have to possess before we can give. Those who have the mission of giving to others must grow first in the knowledge of God.

ALBANIA   An eastern European country that in 1912 declared its independence from the Turks, who had occupied it for five centuries. In 1944, the Albanian Communist Party came to power and held the country in repressive isolation until 1985.

ARCHBISHOP   Bishops are Catholic priests who have the authority to ordain, teach, and govern other priests; an archbishop has authority over the bishops, priests, and nuns within a small area, called an archdiocese.

CATHOLIC   Belonging to the Catholic Church, a Christian community with the bishop of Rome, the pope, as its head, and believing in the Catholic faith, a religion centered upon the life and teachings of Jesus Christ.

COMMUNISM   A system of social, political, and economic organization in which all property is owned by the community as a whole; in practice, it is often a system of government dominated by a single party.

LEPERS   People with leprosy, a chronic, mildly infectious disease that frequently leads to amputations. Lepers are often viewed with fear and distaste. The disease has been wiped out throughout most of the developed world.

LORETO   A Catholic institute of nuns dedicated to educating the wealthy and the poor alike, founded in the 17th century in Ireland. The order continues to have a worldwide presence today.

MAHATMA GANDHI   A Hindu religious leader, social reformer, and proponent of nonviolent resistance who is widely credited with Indian independence from Britain.

MISSIONARY   A person sent to a certain area by a religious organization, usually to convert people or to carry out educational or medical work.

MUSLIM   Belonging to Islam, a religion founded by the prophet Muhammad in the seventh century and centered upon the writings in the Koran, which teach absolute submission to a unique and personal god, Allah.

NOBEL PEACE PRIZE   An award established in 1901 by Swedish philanthropist Alfred B. Nobel and given annually in recognition of outstanding achievement in the promotion of peace; past winners have included Martin Luther King Jr. and Nelson Mandela.

NOVICE   A person undergoing the trial and training period of an order of nuns. At the end of this period, the novice either leaves the order or takes the initial, temporary vows of chastity, poverty, and obedience.

POPE JOHN PAUL II   The pope is the bishop of Rome and head of all other bishops, and thus the head of the Catholic Church; John Paul II, born in Poland in 1920, became Pope in 1978.

PURGATORY   The state or condition of souls after death who still need to atone for their sins before they are admitted to heaven, according to the Catholic faith.

VOCATION   A call from God to holiness and to a particular place in the Catholic Church, such as the life of a priest or nun.